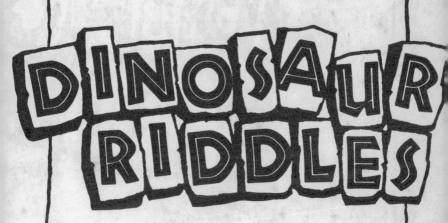

DINOSAUR RIDDLES

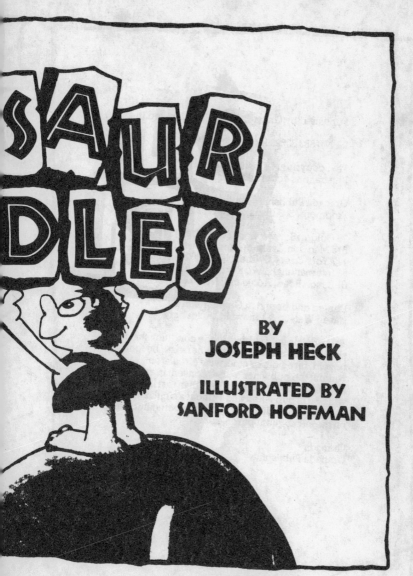

BY
JOSEPH HECK

ILLUSTRATED BY
SANFORD HOFFMAN

A DRAGON BOOK

GRANADA
London Toronto Sydney New York

Published by Granada Publishing Limited in 1983

ISBN 0 583 30620 9

Granada Publishing Limited
Frogmore, St Albans, Herts AL2 2NF
and
36 Golden Square, London W1R 4AH
515 Madison Avenue, New York, NY 10022, USA
117 York Street, Sydney, NSW 2000, Australia
60 International Blvd, Rexdale, Ontario R9W 6J2, Canada
61 Beach Road, Auckland, New Zealand

Printed and bound in Great Britain by
Hazell Watson & Viney Ltd, Aylesbury

Granada ®
Granada Publishing ®

DINOSAUR RIDDLES

How do the giant dinosaurs greet each other?
"Small world, isn't it?"

How do you fit five dinosaurs in a
  Volkswagen?
*Two in front, two in back, and one in the glove
  compartment.*

Who won the dinosaur beauty contest?
No one.

How did the cook get the dinosaur into the
   frying pan?
He used shortening.

What happens when a banana sees a
   dinosaur?
The banana splits.

How do you make a strawberry shake?
Show it a dinosaur.

Why was the dinosaur afraid when it
   swallowed the frog?
It thought it would croak.

Who saw the dinosaur go into the restaurant?
The diners saw.

How do you make a dinosaur stew?
Keep it waiting for two hours.

Why does a Tyrannosaurus eat raw meat?
Because it doesn't know how to cook.

How do you make a
 dinosaur float?
*First take two scoops of ice
cream, add root beer, and then
drop in a small dinosaur.*

How do dinosaurs kiss?
Carefully!

Why are two dinosaurs like a fruit?
Because they are a pair.

When do dinosaurs have two heads, eight
    legs, and two tails?
When there are two of them.

What do dinosaurs have that no other
  animals have?
Baby dinosaurs.

Why are 50-foot high dinosaurs good at telling
the weather?
Because they are the first to know if it rains.

What kind of bird can lift a dinosaur?
A crane.

What would you get if you crossed a dinosaur and a rooster?
The biggest cluck in town.

What would you get if you crossed a 50-foot high dinosaur and a rooster?
An animal that wakes people who live on the top floor.

What would you get if you crossed a dinosaur
  and an owl?
An animal that eats everything it sees but
  doesn't give a hoot.

What would you get if
  you crossed a dinosaur
  and the Abominable
  Snowman?
Frostbite.

What would you get if you crossed a lemon
  and a dinosaur?
A dino-sour.

What would you get if you crossed a dinosaur
    and a rabbit?
     Whatever you would call it, you would
     have hundreds in a month.

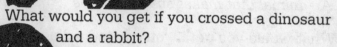

19

What would you get if you crossed a dinosaur
  and a rubber band?
An animal that makes snap decisions.

What would you get if you crossed a dinosaur
  and a computer?
The biggest know-it-all around.

What do you get if you cross a dinosaur and a
  skunk?
The biggest stinker you ever saw.

What do you get if you cross a dinosaur, an
  onion, and an owl?
*An animal that has bad breath but doesn't
  give a hoot.*

What would you get if you crossed a hungry
  dinosaur and a herd of cows?
A dinosaur that wasn't hungry any more.

21

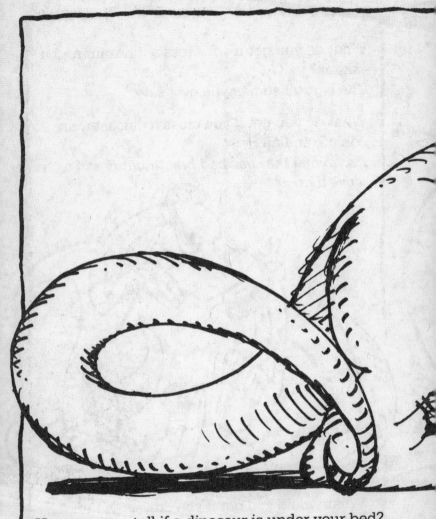

How can you tell if a dinosaur is under your bed?
Your nose is close to the ceiling.

What does a dinosaur call when he loses his
  big toe?
A big toe truck.

What do you call a dinosaur who hitchhikes?
A two-and-a-half ton pickup.

What goes, "Thump, thump, thump, squish.
 Thump, thump, thump, squish."?
A dinosaur with a wet sneaker.

When does a 50-ton dinosaur laugh?
Anytime it wants to.

What would you get if you crossed a popular
  musician and a Tyrannosaurus?
Rockjaw.

Why are elephants like dinosaurs?
Neither can play tennis.

On what do dinosaurs jog?
On dinosaur tracks.

Why can't a dinosaur ride a bicycle?
Because it doesn't have a thumb to ring the bell.

What is worse than a Brontosaurus with a
   sore throat?
A Tyrannosaurus with a toothache.

If a Tyrannosaurus met Count Dracula, what
   would they argue about?
Who would get the first bite.

Igor: If there were a live Tyrannosaurus here, would you like to see me put my head into its mouth?

Boris: *Yes, I would.*

Igor: And I thought you were a friend of mine!

If you had a gun and a Tyrannosaurus came at you from one direction and a Brontosaurus came at you from the other, which one would you shoot?

I'd shoot the gun.

What would you call a Tyrannosaurus Rex from Texas?
A Tyrannosaurus Tex.

What kind of dinosaur do you find in a rodeo?
A bronco-saurus.

A THREE ACT TRAGEDY

Act I: Tyrannosaurus rex and two small dinosaurs.

Act II: Tyrannosaurus rex and one small dinosaur.

Act III: Tyrannosaurus rex.

Would you rather have a Tyrannosaurus or a Triceratops attack you?

I'd rather have them attack each other.

What would you call a pair of Tyrannosaurus Rexes?
A gruesome twosome.

What would you get if two Tyrannosaurus Rexes crashed into each other?
Tyrannosaurus wrecks.

Why is a Tyrannosaurus like a river?
Both have big mouths.

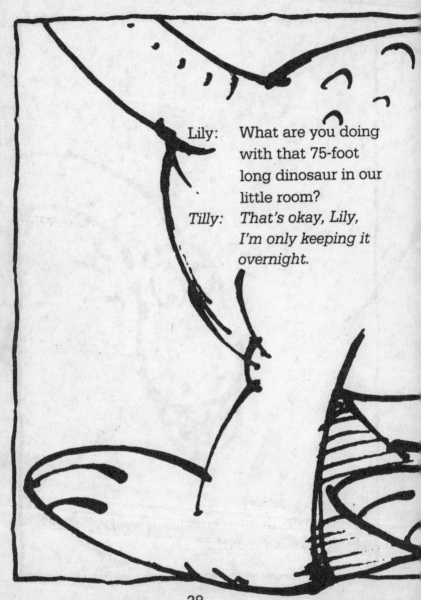

Lily: What are you doing with that 75-foot long dinosaur in our little room?

Tilly: *That's okay, Lily, I'm only keeping it overnight.*

Why is it good to tell stories about ferocious
dinosaurs in hot weather?
Because they are so chilling.

What is the best way to talk to a dinosaur?
By long distance.

What kind of fur do you get from a dinosaur?
As fur as you can get.

If three dinosaurs are a crowd, what are four
  and five?
Nine.

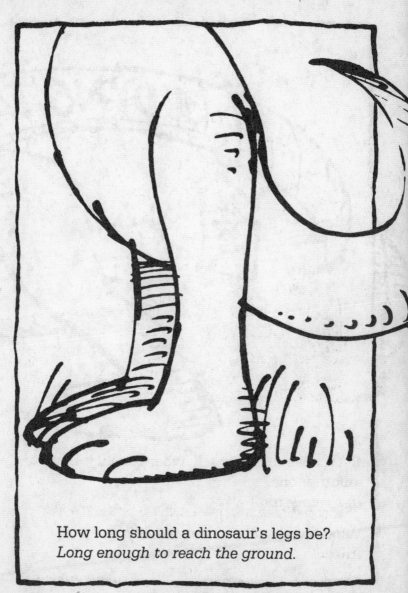

How long should a dinosaur's legs be?
Long enough to reach the ground.

If a dinosaur lost its tail, where could it buy another one?
In a retail store.

What always follows a dinosaur?
Its tail.

Which dinosaur eats with its tail?
They all do. Dinosaurs don't take off their tails when they eat.

Why did the dinosaur chase its tail?
It was trying to make ends meet.

Why shouldn't you step on a dinosaur's tail?
It may only be his tail, but it could be your end.

What did the small dinosaur say when the big
dinosaur bit its tail?
"That's the end of me!"

First scientist:	The expedition is sending us some dinosaur tails.
Second scientist:	*Dinosaur tails? I never heard of anything so ridiculous.*
First scientist:	Well, read this telegram for yourself: "Just found some dinosaur skeletons. Sending details tomorrow."

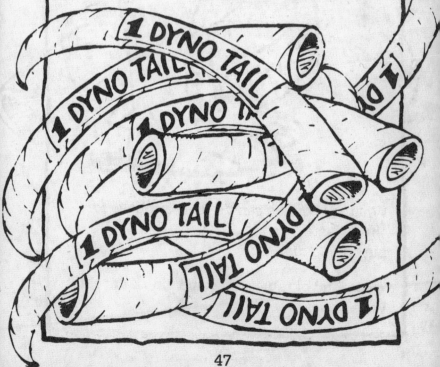

What two things can't a dinosaur have for
  breakfast?
Lunch and dinner.

What kind of tables did some dinosaurs eat?
Vege-tables.

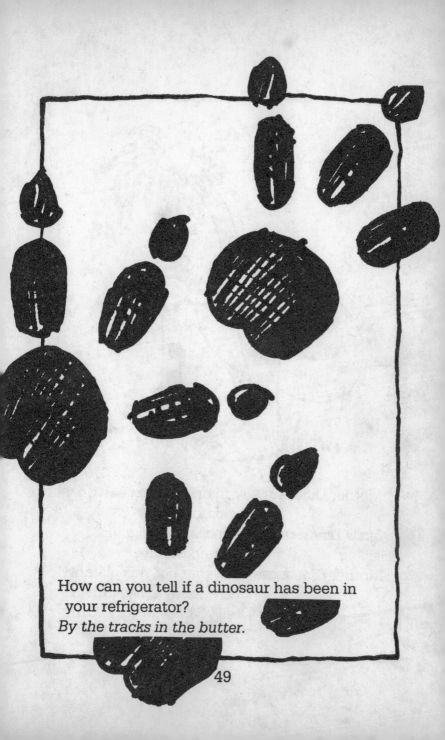

How can you tell if a dinosaur has been in your refrigerator?
By the tracks in the butter.

Mother Dinosaur: Junior, what on earth are you doing?

Little Dinosaur: *I'm chasing an animal around the tree.*

Mother Dinosaur: Cut that out this instant! How many times must I tell you not to play with your food?

What do you do with a blue dinosaur?
Cheer him up.

What color is a ferocious dinosaur?
G'way!

What do you do with a green dinosaur?
Wait until he ripens.

Ike: "I just swallowed a dinosaur bone."
Mike: *"Are you choking?"*
Ike: "No, I'm serious."

Did you hear the joke about the dog who
  choked on a dinosaur bone?
Never mind, you wouldn't be able to swallow
  it either.

Mindy: Do you know the difference between
       a piece of candy and a dinosaur
       bone?
Cindy: *No.*
Mindy: Good, then eat this dinosaur bone.

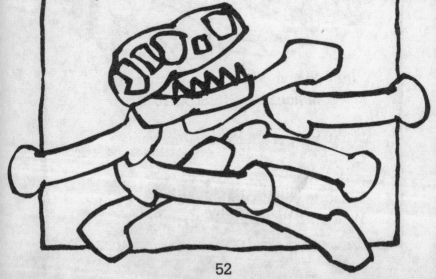

A Poem: A PLESIOSAURUS

There once was a Plesiosaurus
Which did live when the earth was porous.
  But it fainted with shame
  When it first heard its name,
And departed long ages before us.

What is worse than one hungry dinosaur?
Two hungry dinosaurs.

What amazing thing did the thirsty
   dinosaur do?
It drank Canada Dry.

What is 10 dinosaurs + 5 dinosaurs minus 15 dinosaurs?

What is 3 dinosaurs + 6 dinosaurs minus 9 dinosaurs?

What is 17 dinosaurs + 3 dinosaurs minus 20 dinosaurs?

All that work for nothing!

What would you get if you crossed a dinosaur
and the Invisible Man?
I don't know what you would call it, but it
wouldn't be much to look at.

Doctor: Why are you snapping your fingers?
Patient: *To keep the dinosaurs away.*
Doctor: That's silly.
Patient: *(still snapping his fingers). No it isn't.*
           Have you seen any dinosaurs around
           lately?
Doctor: No, I haven't.
Patient: *See, it works.*

What has four legs like a dinosaur, a head like a dinosaur, a body like a dinosaur, a tail like a dinosaur, looks like a dinosaur—but isn't a dinosaur?
A picture of a dinosaur.

Did you hear about the Tyrannosaurus who went to Hollywood?
All he could get was bit parts.

Abe: What do you get if you tell a joke
about a 25-ton dinosaur?

Gabe: *Big laughs?*

Abe: Right!
What do you get if you tell a joke
about a 75-ton dinosaur?

Gabe: *Bigger laughs?*

Abe: Right!
What do you get if you tell a joke
about a 200-ton dinosaur?

Gabe: *Still bigger laughs?*

Abe: Wrong! They don't come in that size.

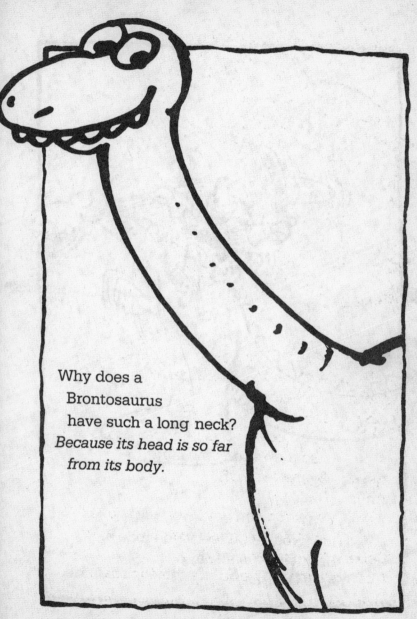

Why does a
  Brontosaurus
  have such a long neck?
*Because its head is so far
  from its body.*

How would you feel if you rode a
  Brontosaurus all day?
Saddle saurus.

When is a dinosaur like a creature from outer space?
When it is Martian along.

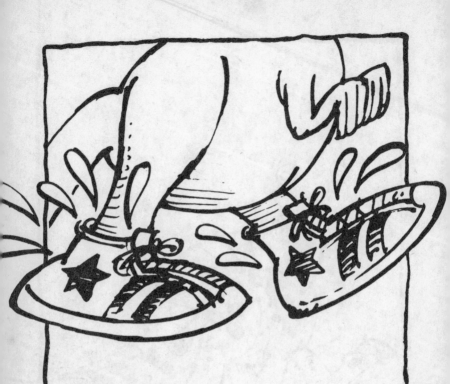

What does a dinosaur get if it crosses a stream
  and a brook?
Wet feet.

What did the little stream say when the
  dinosaur sat in it?
"Well I'll be dammed!"

Why do dinosaurs lie down when they sleep?
Because they can't lie up.

What is the difference between a dinosaur
   and a toothpick?
*Well, if you don't know, you'd better not pick
your teeth.*

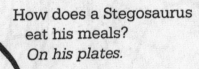

How does a Stegosaurus
   eat his meals?
On his plates.

Why wouldn't a Tyrannosaurus be a good
   neighbor?
*Because he would always be stopping in for a
bite.*

What song does a Tyrannosaurus sing at
   Christmas?
"I'm screaming of a bite Christmas . . ."

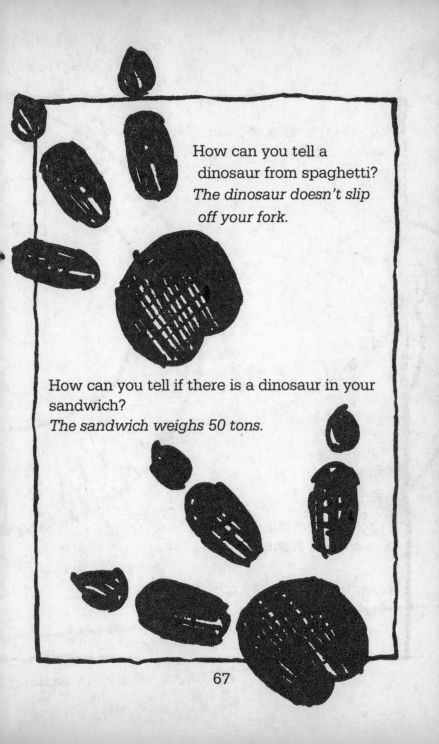

How can you tell a
dinosaur from spaghetti?
*The dinosaur doesn't slip
off your fork.*

How can you tell if there is a dinosaur in your
sandwich?
The sandwich weighs 50 tons.

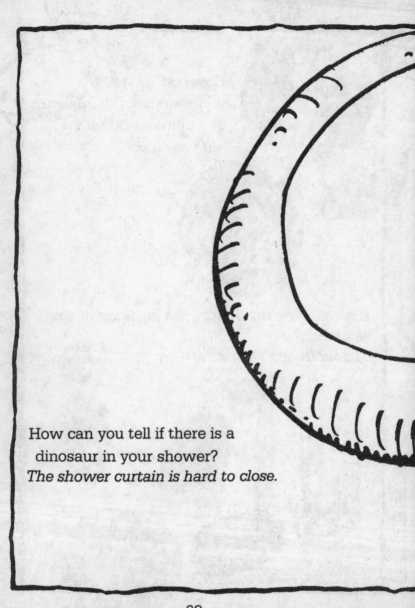

How can you tell if there is a
dinosaur in your shower?
The shower curtain is hard to close.

What is a dinosaur after it is 40 years old?
41 years old.

What do you do with a dinosaur when it is 41
years old?
Wish it a happy birthday.

What do you call a dinosaur
that makes more footprints
than any other dinosaur?
A track star.

Which dinosaur can jump higher than a
  house?
All dinosaurs can. What house can jump?

What is 50 feet long and jumps every two
  seconds?
A dinosaur with hiccups.

What happened to the tree when it saw the
dinosaur?
It became petrified.

Why did the dinosaur cross
   the road?
To prove he wasn't chicken.

Why did the dinosaur
   cross the road and
   cross back again?
*Because he was a
   double-crosser.*

Why did the dinosaur cross
   the road, roll in the mud,
   and cross back again?
*Because he was a dirty
   double-crosser.*

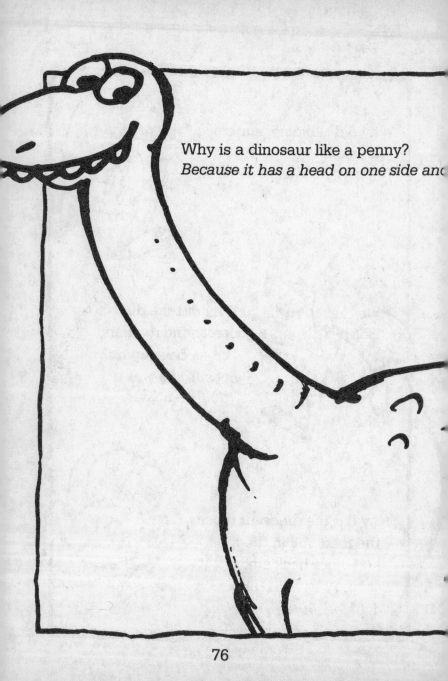

Why is a dinosaur like a penny?
Because it has a head on one side and

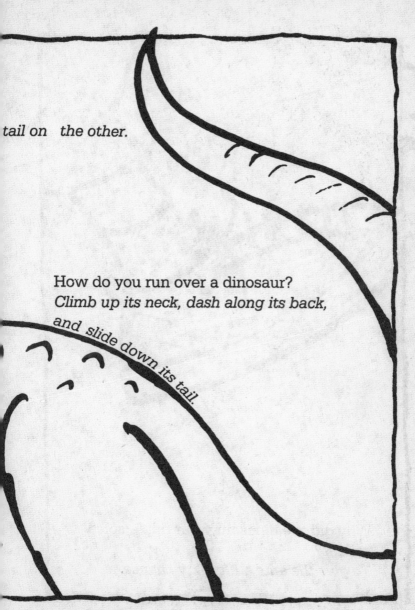

tail on   the other.

How do you run over a dinosaur?
Climb up its neck, dash along its back,
and slide down its tail.

Why did the dinosaur wear ripple-soled
  shoes?
To give the ants a fifty-fifty chance.

Imagine you are on an island filled with
dinosaurs and have no way to escape—
what should you do?
Quit imagining.

What kind of words should you use when you talk to a dinosaur?
Big ones.

What would you get if you crossed a dinosaur
  and a canary?
*I don't know what you'd call it, but when it
  sings you'd better listen.*

What would you get if you crossed a dinosaur
  and a parrot?
*I don't know what you'd call it, but if it asks
  for a cracker, you'd better give it the whole
  box. And watch out, or it'll talk your ear off.*

How do you get down from a dinosaur?
You don't get down from a dinosaur, you get down from a duck.

What should you watch if you meet a dinosaur?
Your step.

Why did the Tyrannosaurus go to the dentist?
For its bite.

What time is it when a Tyrannosaurus has
cavities?
Tooth-hurty.

What do you have if a herd of dinosaurs walks
   through a potato field?
Mashed potatoes.

If you were walking through a swamp and
   saw a Tyrannosaurus, what time would it be?
Time to run.

When you dream about dinosaurs attacking
   you, what horse do you see?
A night-mare.

What happens if a herd of dinosaurs runs over
  Batman and Robin?
Flatman and Ribbon.

How do you blow a dinosaur up?
With dino-mite.

What note do you hear when a dinosaur falls
  down a coal mine?
A-flat minor.

There was a movie so old on TV the other day that the cowboy was riding a dinosaur.

What should you do if a dinosaur charges you?
Better pay him.

How do you keep a Triceratops from charging?
Take away its credit cards.

What is better than presence of mind when
   you meet a dinosaur?
Absence of body.

Where did dinosaurs leave their spaceships?
At parking meteors.

What are you when you meet a BIG dinosaur?
You are in BIG trouble.

Where do they sell dinosaurs?
In a dino-store.

Why is it easy to weigh dinosaurs?
Because they have their own scales.

What weighs 50 tons, has huge teeth, lived
  millions of years ago, and is blue?
A dinosaur holding its breath.

What weighs 50 tons, has huge teeth, lived millions of years ago, and has a red nose?
Rudolph, the red-nosed dinosaur.

Museum Guide:	That dinosaur in the glass case is seventy million and six years old.
Visitor:	*That's amazing! But how can you date it so exactly?*
Museum Guide:	Well, I've been working here six years, and it was seventy million years old when I started.

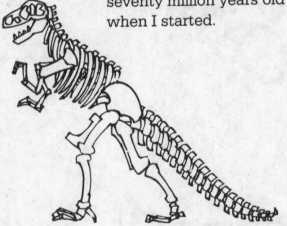

Joe:	I just saw a dinosaur in the zoo.
Moe:	*Dinosaurs have been extinct for millions of years. Who ever heard of dinosaurs in the zoo?*
Joe:	You did. I just told you.

Lem: Want to hear a dirty joke?

Clem: *Sure.*

Lem: A dinosaur fell in the mud.

Lem: Want to hear a clean joke?

Clem: *Sure.*

Lem: Then he fell in the lake.

95

What is as big as a dinosaur but weighs nothing?
The shadow of a dinosaur.

Where would you look for a dinosaur after a
  heavy rain?
In a dino-sewer.

If a dinosaur dug a hole 10 feet deep and 10
  feet across, how much dirt would there be
  in the hole?
None. A hole is empty.

What does a hippie call a dinosaur skeleton?
Deady-oh!

Did you hear the joke about the dinosaur that
  was buried in a deep hole?
Never mind, you wouldn't be able to dig it.

Did you hear the joke
   about the dinosaur?
*Never mind, you would
   only laugh at it.*

If a dinosaur dined on dainty dates, how many
   D's are there in all?
None. There are no Ds in "all."

What do you say when you meet a two-
  headed dinosaur?
"Hello, hello!"

What happens when a dinosaur steps on your ankle?
You get Ankylosaurus.

Why is a dinosaur who walks along the beach like Christmas?
Because it gets Sandy Claws.

How would a tailor make a suit the right size for a dinosaur?
Make the dinosaur so angry he has a fit.

Why did the lemon run away from the dinosaur?
Because it was yellow.

Flip: What is the difference between a lemon, a dinosaur, and a bottle of glue?

Flop: *I give up. What is the difference?*

Flip: You can swallow a lemon, but you can't swallow a dinosaur.

Flop: *What about the bottle of glue?*

Flip: I just threw that in to stick you.

Why was the dinosaur skeleton a coward?
Because it had no guts.

Why are dinosaur skeletons like donuts?
Both have nothing in the middle.

How do you serve food to a dinosaur skeleton?
On bone china.

Tip: I wish I had a million dollars to buy a dinosaur.

Top: *Why do you want a dinosaur?*

Tip: No reason. I just want the million dollars.

Joe: What is the difference between a dinosaur and a snew?

Moe: *What's a snew?*

Joe: Nothing much. What's snew with you?

What would happen if a dinosaur sat in front
  of you at the movies?
You would miss most of the show.

How do you order a Brontosaurus to come to
  you?
"Pronto, Saurus!"

Why couldn't the dinosaur go to the dance?
It didn't have any body to go with.

On what do dinosaurs play in the schoolyard?
On dino-see-saurs.

What happened when the dinosaur took the road to town?
The police made him bring it back.

What kind of injury do you get from touching
  a dinosaur?
A dino-sore.

How do you cut a dinosaur in half?
With a dino-saw.

What do you call a person who sticks his right
  arm down a dinosaur's throat?
"Lefty."

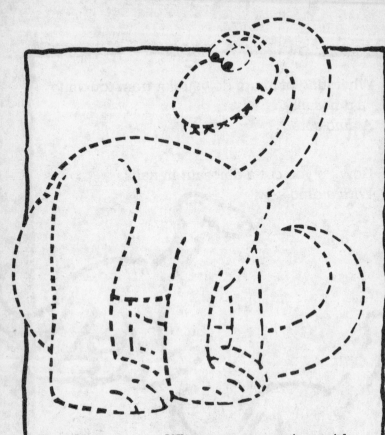

First Hunter: Where are you going with that rifle?

Second Hunter: Hunting for dinosaurs.

First Hunter: But there are no dinosaurs around here.

Second Hunter: I know that. If there were any, I wouldn't have to hunt for them.

Why can't dinosaurs play hide-and-seek
  around a mountain?
Because the mountain peaks.

Stu: I can lift a dinosaur with one hand.
Lou: *I don't believe you.*
Stu: Get me a dinosaur with one hand, and
       I'll show you.

What weighs 50 tons and has sixteen wheels?
A dinosaur on roller skates.

What time is it when a dinosaur sits on a
 clock?
Time to get a new clock.

Why is a dinosaur like a grandfather clock?
Both are old-timers.

When do dinosaurs annoy most?
When they get under your skin.

If five dinosaurs were attacking one dinosaur,
 what time would it be?
Five after one.

If a dinosaur loses a hand, where can it buy
 another one?
In a second hand store.

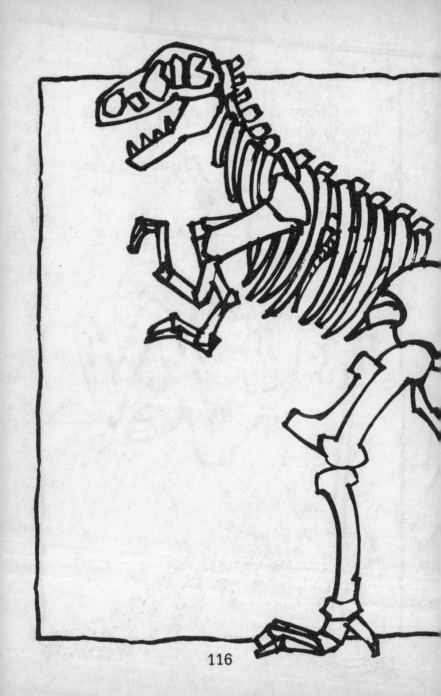

How many dinosaurs can you put in an empty museum?
One. After that the museum isn't empty any more.

How do you make a dinosaur skeleton laugh?
Tickle its funny bone.

How do you clean a dinosaur skeleton?
With a skeleton crew.

Why are dinosaur skeletons silly?
Because they are so empty-headed.

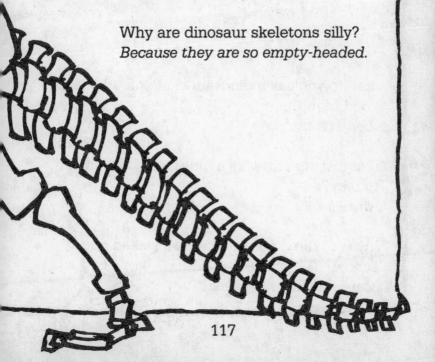

117

What do you call a dinosaur skeleton who is a
good friend?
A bony crony.

What instrument does a dinosaur skeleton like
to play?
A trom-bone.

Why was the dinosaur skeleton kicked out of
school?
Because it was a bonehead.

Why are dinosaur skeletons like blank
  applications?
Because their forms are not filled out.

What dinosaur weighs 2,000 pounds and is all
  bone?
A dinosaur skele-ton.

Abe:　My father has the biggest job in the
　　　museum.
Gabe: What does he do?
Abe:　He dusts the dinosaurs.

What do you call a dinosaur skeleton that
  sleeps all day?
Lazy bones.

If a dinosaur skeleton rang your bell, what
  would you have?
A dead ringer.

How did they ship dinosaur skeletons in the
  Old West?
By Bony Express.

Why did the scientist pour milk on the
dinosaur skeleton?
He heard that milk was good for the bones.

Why didn't the dinosaur skeleton like being in
the museum?
Because his heart wasn't in it.

How did the dinosaur feel after standing all
day in the museum?
Dead on its feet.

Why are dinosaur skeletons far out?
Because they are the living end.

What do people who dig up dinosaurs talk about?
Old times.

Nit: My father collects dinosaur bones. He has a rare Brontosaurus leg bone.

Wit: *That's nothing. My father has an Adam's apple.*

What did the hippie fossil hunter say to the dinosaur?
"I dig you."

In what room won't you find a dinosaur
  skeleton?
A living room.

Why don't dinosaur skeletons like to dance
  all night?

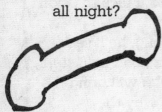

        Because they feel dead
          the next day.

There once was a young man named Jones
Who was fond of dinosaur bones.
   After eating a score,
   He asked for some more,
That's why he lies under these stones.

A famous dinosaur hunter was asked how he planned to catch a herd of dinosaurs. "It's simple," he said. "The first thing I do when I'm in dinosaur country is to find a water hole. I take out my dinosaur kit, which consists of a pencil, paper, tacks, milk bottle, binoculars, and a pair of tweezers. I then make a sign on which I write FOR DINOSORES. I tack the sign up on a tree and then I wait.

"When a dinosaur comes along, he'll see that 'dinosore' is spelled wrong, and he'll start laughing. The sound of laughing will bring the other dinosaurs nearby to see why the dinosaur is laughing.

"When there are a whole bunch of dinosaurs, I look at them through the wrong end of the binoculars. This will make them tiny. Then I pick up the dinosaurs with my tweezers and drop them into the milk bottle."

What would you get if you crossed a Tyrannosaurus and a witch?
A Tyrannosaurus hex.

Who started all the dinosaur riddles and
jokes?

—*That's what the dinosaurs want to know.*